ISBN-10: 1537105221

ISBN-13: 978-1537105222

Contents

Introduction

Dads love telling jokes.

We like to think of ourselves as the comedians
(or clowns!) of the family, and we especially love
making our kids laugh.

But being a funny parent is difficult!

We go though a lot of our lives being able to make
jokes without many restrictions and often these jokes
can stray away from family-friendly material!

Suddenly we're presented with a new, unfamiliar
audience, with whom sarcasm and innuendos are
totally inappropriate.

We want to make happy, friendly and innocent jokes
that the whole family can enjoy, and what we're left
with is silliness, corny jokes and awful puns!

This situation has created what has recently become
known as the 'Dad Joke'.

This book celebrates this hilariously facepalm and
groan-inducing style of joke!

Jokes

— 1 —

Do you want to hear a joke about paper?

Actually nevermind, it's *tearable*!

— 2 —

What do you call a fish with no eyes?

A *fshhhh*!

— 3 —

What was the only thing left after the French
cheese factory exploded?

De Brie!

— 4 —

What did the person who invented the
knock knock joke win?

The *Nobel* prize!

— 5 —

What's an "oying?"

This joke!

— 6 —

Why are Saturday and Sunday the strongest days?

The rest are *weak*-days!

— 7 —

What does a vegetarian zombie say?

***Grrraaains*!**

— 8 —

Why didn't the dad recognize the vegetarian girl?

Because he hadn't met *herbivore*!

— 9 —

What do you call a dangerous Italian restaurant?

The *Spaghetto*!

— 10 —

Why do scuba divers fall backwards
into the water?

**Because if they fell forwards they'd *still*
be in the boat!**

— 11 —

What do you call a fly without wings?

A *walk*!

— 12 —

Is it safe to dive into swimming pools?

It *deep ends*!

— 13 —

Why did the dad get fired from his job
at the calendar factory?

He took a few days off!

— 14 —

What's the difference between a badly dressed man on a tricycle and a well dressed man on a bicycle?

Attire!

— 15 —

What did the pirate say on his 80th birthday?

Aye Matey!

– 16 –

How do you feel when you run out of coffee?

Depresso.

– 17 –

Did you know diarrhea is hereditary?

It *runs* in your *jeans*!

— 18 —

What was wrong will the sick cat?

He wasn't *feline* well!

— 19 —

What do you call a belt made out of watches?

A *waist* of time!

— 20 —

What's the worst thing about sleeping
like a log?

Waking up in the fireplace!

— 21 —

What's red and smells like blue paint?

Red Paint!

— 22 —

What do you call a nosy pepper?

Jalapeno **business!**

— 23 —

Why should you never trust an atom?

They make everything up!

— 24 —

Why wasn't the mushroom allowed
to host the party?

There wasn't *much-room*!

— 25 —

Did you hear about the two antennas
that got married?

The *reception* was amazing!

— 26 —

Did you hear that David lost his ID on holiday?

Now we have to call him *Dav*!

— 27 —

Why should you not write with a dull pencil?

Because it's *pointless*.

— 28 —

Why did the detective go to the
Mexican restaurant?

He was looking for a *case-idea*!

— 29 —

How did Darth Vader know what Luke got
him for Christmas?

He felt his *presents*!

— 30 —

Why can't you hear a pterodactyl
go to the toilet?

The "P" is silent!

— 31 —

What did the hat say to the hat rack?

You stay here I'll go on *ahead*!

— 32 —

What did the ocean and the sea say
to each other?

Nothing, they just *waved*!

— 33 —

How many apples grow on a tree?

All of them!

— 34 —

Why doesn't anybody like jokes
about sausages?

They're the *wurst*!

— 35 —

How did the dad feel after he ate
gone-off seafood?

A little *eel*!

— 36 —

Why couldn't the bicycle stand up by itself?

It was *two tired*!

— 37 —

How does a penguin build its house?

Igloos it together!

— 38 —

What's the best way to carve wood?

Whittle by whittle!

— 39 —

What is life without geometry?

Pointless!

— 40 —

What do you call a short psychic
that's escaped from jail?

A small medium at large!

— 41 —

What kind of dinosaur has the
biggest vocabulary?

A *Thesaurus!*

— 42 —

Can February March?

No, but *April May!*

— 43 —

How do you cook toilet paper?

Brown it and then throw it in the pot!

— 44 —

Why should you hold open the door
for a clown?

It's a nice *jester*!

— 45 —

When should you worry about
swimming in milk?

When it's *past your eyes*!

— 46 —

Who takes the second shot in a
game of snooker?

Find out after *the break!*

— 47 —

Why is it hard to joke around with thieves?

They always *take things literally*!

— 48 —

Two peanuts were walking down the street..

One was *assaulted*!

— 49 —

What do you call a group of whales
playing instruments?

An *Orca-stra*!

— 50 —

Why didn't the dad put the cat out?

It wasn't on fire!

— 51 —

Did you hear about the crazy bug
on the moon?

It's a *lunar-tic*!

— 52 —

Why did the can-crusher quit his job?

Because it was *soda-pressing*!

— 53 —

What is ET short for?

He only has little legs!

— 54 —

What do you call a guy with a rubber toe?

Roberto!

— 55 —

What do you do when there's a sink standing outside your door?

Just let that *sink in for a moment*!

— 56 —

Which side of a chicken has more feathers?

The *out*side!

— 57 —

Where do cows go for a first date?

The *moovies!*

— 58 —

Why do seagulls live by the sea?

**Because if they lived by bays
they'd be *bagels*!**

— 59 —

What should you do if you see
a space man?

Park the car, man!

— 60 —

Why did the cookie cry?

His mother was a *wafer* too long!

— 61 —

What did the slow tomato say to
the quick tomato?

I'll *ketch* up!

— 62 —

Why didn't the dad buy camouflage pants?

He couldn't find any!

— 63 —

What did sushi A say to sushi B?

Wasa-b!

— 64 —

What do you call a lawn statue with a
good sense of rhythm?

A *metro-gnome!*

— 65 —

Why do bears have hairy coats?

Fur protection!

— 66 —

How do prisoners call each other?

With their *cell* phones!

— 67 —

Why did the Cyclops have to close
his school?

He only had one *pupil*!

— 68 —

What kind of magic do cows believe in?

*Moo*doo!

— 69 —

What do you get if you cross a vampire
with a snowman?

Frostbite!

— 70 —

What does a cloud wear under its shorts?

*Thunder*pants!

— 71 —

What do you call a blind dinosaur?

Doyouthinkhesaurus!

— 72 —

Why did the baby miss its umbilical chord?

It grew *attached* to it!

— 73 —

What did the red light say to the green light?

Don't look, I'm *changing*!

— 74 —

Why do bees hum?

They don't know the words!

— 75 —

Why did the scarecrow win an award?

He was *outstanding in his field*!

— 76 —

What kind of candy is never on time?

Choco-*late!*

— 77 —

What do you call a fake noodle?

An *impasta*!

— 78 —

Why did the train driver get struck
by lightning?

He was a good *conductor*!

— 79 —

Why did Cinderella get kicked off the
soccer team?

Because she kept *running from the ball!*

— 80 —

What is a mummies favourite
genre of music?

Wrap music!

— 81 —

Why are dry erase boards so great?

They're **remarkable**!

— 82 —

Why should you be suspicious of trees?

They're very *shady*!

— 83 —

What do you call a woman with one leg
longer than the other?

***Eileen*!**

— 84 —

What did the dad who was scared of elevators do?

He took *steps* to avoid them!

— 85 —

What's orange and sounds like a parrot?

A *carrot!*

— 86 —

How do you make a glow worm happy?

Cut off it's tail.. it will be *delighted*!

— 87 —

What would bears be without bees?

***Ears*!**

— 88 —

What happened when the red boat crashed
into the blue boat?

The sailors were *marooned*!

— 89 —

What happens when you put a sheep
on a trampoline?

You get a *woolly jumper*!

— 90 —

Why should you take a backpack with
you to choir practice?

To *carry your tune!*

— 91 —

What did the beaver say to the old tree?

It's been nice *gnawing* you!

— 92 —

What did the shy pebble wish for?

To be a little *boulder*!

— 93 —

Two beers are playing basketball,
which one wins?

The one with more *hops*!

— 94 —

What do you call a man who can't find his car?

Carlos!

— 95 —

What's the difference between tune
and a piano?

**You can tune a piano but you can't
piano a tuna!**

— 96 —

How do you make holy water?

You boil the *hell* out of it!

— 97 —

What happened to the dad who fell in love
during a backflip?

He was *heels over head*!

— 98 —

What did the sailor say to the 2x4?

Welcome *a board*!

— 99 —

What happened when the corduroy pillow
was invented?

It made *headlines*!

— 100 —

How do you organize a space party?

You *planet*!

— 101 —

What do you call a can opener that doesn't work?

A *can't* opener!

— 102 —

What do you call a detective alligator that
wears a vest?

An *investigator*!

— 103 —

What did the Lion King tell Simba when he was
walking too slow?

Mufasa!

— 104 —

What's the best thing about living
in Switzerland?

I don't know, but their flag is a *big plus*!

— 105 —

What didn't the melons get married?

Because they *cantaloupe*!

— 106 —

Why can't a nose be 12 inches long?

Because then it would be a *foot*!

— 107 —

How do you make a tissue dance?

You put a little *boogie* in it!

— 108 —

Why do gorillas have big nostrils?

Because they have big *fingers*!

— 109 —

Why doesn't anybody enjoy spending time
with little Russian dolls?

They're *full of themselves*!

— 110 —

Where do Volkswagens go when they get old?

The Old *Volks* home!

— 111 —

What sound does a nut make when it sneezes?

Cashew!

— 112 —

What does it mean if you have a
bladder infection?

Urine trouble!

— 113 —

Why do vampires believe everything
you tell them?

Because they're *suckers*!

— 114 —

What do you call twins who live together?

Womb-mates!

— 115 —

Why did the coffee call the police?

Because it got *mugged!*

— 116 —

How does Moses make tea?

Hebrews it!

— 117 —

What do you call a guy with no shins?

Tony!

— 118 —

What did the big chimney say to the
little chimney?

You're too young to be smoking!

— 119 —

What do you call a snobbish prisoner going
down the stairs?

A condescending *con descending*!

— 120 —

What do you call a fat psychic?

A *four-chin* teller!

— 121 —

What's slow, large, grey and doesn't matter?

An *irrelephant!*

— 122 —

What kind of pictures do turtles take?

Shellfies!

— 123 —

Why are skeletons so calm?

Because nothing gets *under their skin!*

— 124 —

How many tickles does it take to make
an octopus laugh?

Tentacles!

— 125 —

What's the difference between Dubai
and Abu Dhabi?

**People from Dubai don't like the Flintstones
and people from *Abu Dhabi Do!***

— 126 —

What do sprinters eat before a race?

Nothing, they *fast!*

— 127 —

What happened to the sick Italian chef?

He *pasta*-way!

— 128 —

What do you call a teacher who never breaks
wind in public?

A *private tutor!*

— 129 —

Why was the graveyard overcrowded?

People were *dying to get in!*

— 130 —

My doctor said I'm only allowed to eat tropical fruit from now on..

It's enough to make a *mango* crazy!

— 131 —

Why don't blind people go skydiving?

It scares their dogs too much!

— 132 —

Why shouldn't you buy anything
made with Velcro?

It's a *rip-off!*

— 133 —

What did the romantic finger say
to the thumb?

I'm in *glove* with you!

— 134 —

Why don't crabs give to charity?

They're *shellfish!*

— 135 —

Did you hear about the kidnapping
at the school?

It was okay, he woke up!

— 136 —

If Sherlock lived in America, what would he call primary school?

Elementary, my dear Watson!

— 137 —

Where do you go if you want to learn to make ice cream?

Sunday school!

— 138 —

What did the left eye say to the right eye?

Between you and me, something smells!

— 139 —

Why is conjunctivitis.com such a popular website?

It's a *site for sore eyes!*

— 140 —

What did the grape do when he
got stepped on?

Let out a little *wine!*

— 141 —

What did the 8 say to the 0?

Do you like my belt?

— 142 —

Why doesn't Dracula have many friends?

Because he's a *pain in the neck!*

— 143 —

Why did the A go to the bathroom and come out as an E?

Because he had a *vowel* movement!

— 144 —

What happened to the magical tractor?

It turned into a field!

— 145 —

Why does Piglet smell?

Because he plays with *Pooh*!

— 146 —

What lies at the bottom of the ocean
and twitches?

A nervous wreck!

— 147 —

Why did the tomato blush?

It saw the salad *dressing!*

— 148 —

What did the overly excited gardener do
when spring finally arrived?

He *wet his plants!*

— 149 —

How do you stop bacon from curling
in the pan?

You take away their little brooms!

— 150 —

What do you get if you drop a piano
down a mine shaft?

A *flat miner!*

— 151 —

How do crazy people get through a forest?

They take the *psycho-path!*

— 152 —

Why was the broom late for work?

It *overswept!*

— 153 —

What happened at the nightclub where people
had to bend down to get their drinks?

They had to *raise the bar!*

— 154 —

Why did the dad smear peanut butter
on the road?

To go with the traffic *jam*!

— 155 —

What do you say to get gold's attention?

AU!

— 156 —

Where does batman go to the bathroom?

The *batroom*!

— 157 —

What did the teacher do with the student's cheese report?

He *grated* it!

— 158 —

What do you call a cow with no legs?

Ground beef!

— 159 —

What happened to the frog's car?

It got *toad!*

— 160 —

Why did the dad play soccer even though
he was terrible at it?

For the *kicks*!

— 161 —

What do you call a person with no
body and no nose?

Nobody knows!

— 162 —

What did the mountain climber name his son?

Cliff!

— 163 —

How do snails fight?

They *slug* it out!

— 164 —

Why did the dad read a book on the history
of glue in one sitting?

He couldn't put it down!

— 165 —

Why haven't you heard of the band 1023MB?

They haven't got a *gig* yet!

— 166 —

What did one wall say to the other?

Let's meet on the corner!

— 167 —

What's the difference between an African
elephant and an Indian elephant?

About 5000 miles!

— 168 —

Why did the dad sell his vacuum cleaner?

It was just *collecting up dust!*

— 169 —

What's red and bad for your teeth?

A brick!

— 170 —

What did the dad say when his son broke
my arm in two places?

Stay away from those places!

— 171 —

Where can you buy an ark?

I *Noah* guy!

— 172 —

What's the problem with nightclubs
on the moon?

There's no *atmosphere*!

— 173 —

My boss asked me to attach two
pieces of wood together.

I nailed it!

— 174 —

Why didn't the gun have a job?

He got *fired!*

— 175 —

What do you call a monkey in a minefield?

A *baboom*!

— 176 —

What's the difference between
ignorance and apathy?

I don't know and I don't care!

— 177 —

What are ninja's favourite type of shoes?

Sneakers!

— 178 —

What do you give a sick bird?

Tweetment!

— 179 —

What's brown and sounds like a bell?

Dung!

— 180 —

Why does Superman gets invited to
a lot of dinners?

Because he's a *Supperhero!*

— 181 —

How can you tell if an ant is a boy or a girl?

They're all girls, otherwise they'd be uncles!

— 182 —

What do you call a bear without any teeth?

A *gummy* bear!

— 183 —

What does a baby computer call his father?

Data!

— 184 —

Why does Waldo wear a striped shirt?

Because he doesn't want to be *spotted!*

— 185 —

What did the policeman say to
his belly button?

You're *under a vest!*

— 186 —

Why do ghosts like elevators?

Because they *lift their spirits!*

— 187 —

What did the mother buffalo say to
her boy when he went out?

Bison!

— 188 —

What did Snow White say when she
left the photo booth?

Someday my *prints* will come!

— 189 —

Why didn't the lifeguard save the hippie?

Because he was too *far out!*

— 190 —

What do you call somebody who
points out the obvious?

Somebody who points out the obvious!

— 191 —

What does a clock do when it's hungry?

It goes back *four seconds*!

— 192 —

Why should you give people fridges as gifts?

Because their faces light up when they open them!

— 193 —

What do you call a man leaving a hospital?

Manuel!

— 194 —

I went to the doctor today and he told me I
had type A blood..

But it was a _type O!_

— 195 —

Why do birds fly south for the winter?

Because its too far to walk!

— 196 —

What did the duck say to the bartender?

Put it on my *bill!*

— 197 —

Why did the dad quit the shoe recycling shop?

It was *sole destroying!*

— 198 —

How many lives does a German cat have?

Nein!

— 199 —

Why was the shovel such an
important invention?

It was *ground-breaking!*

— 200 —

Why do you never see elephants
hiding in trees?

Because they're so good at it!

Thank You

Thank you for reading Dad Jokes!

I really hope you've enjoyed reading this book and tormenting your family and friends with these awful jokes!

Please leave a review on Amazon if you have the time!

22315552R00068

Printed in Poland
by Amazon Fulfillment
Poland Sp. z o.o., Wrocław